ELLA
Diaries

TOP SECRET!

Meredith Costain

With special thanks to Cristina, Mewanmi, Gwyneth, Isabel, Ananya and Sucheta from Boroondara Park Primary School—M.C.

For my pirate crew—
Zoe, Jade and Ray—D.M.

Danielle McDonald

Scholastic Australia
345 Pacific Highway Lindfield NSW 2070
An imprint of Scholastic Australia Pty Limited
PO Box 579 Gosford NSW 2250
ABN 11 000 614 577
www.scholastic.com.au

Part of the Scholastic Group
Sydney • Auckland • New York • Toronto • London • Mexico City
• New Delhi • Hong Kong • Buenos Aires • Puerto Rico

Published by Scholastic Australia in 2016.

National Library of Australia Cataloguing-in-Publication entry

Creator: Costain, Meredith, 1955- author.
Title: Friends not forever / Meredith Costain; illustrated by Danielle McDonald.
ISBN: 9781760157173 (paperback)
Series: Costain, Meredith, 1955- Ella diaries; 7
Target Audience: For primary school age.
Subjects: Diaries--Juvenile fiction.
Friendship--Juvenile fiction.
Schools--Juvenile fiction.
Other Creators/Contributors:
McDonald, Danielle, illustrator.
Dewey Number: A823.3

Typeset in Sweetie Pie.

This edition - September 2023
Printed in India at Ram Printograph Delhi

ELLA Diaries

FRIENDS NOT FOREVER

Monday night, in bed, just before lights out

Dear Diary,

TWO very thrilling and mysterious things happened at school today.

Thrilling AND Mysterious THING NUMBER ONE

There is a new girl in our class. Her name is Amethyst Merryweather.

These are the things I know about her:

1. She is VERY quiet.

2. She doesn't like answering questions about herself.

That's it. (Hopefully I will have more to report about this tomorrow. ☺)

Thrilling AND Mysterious THING

NUMBER TWO

Our lovely and excellent teacher Ms Weiss announced that something very excitering is going to be happening at school soon. Something we will LOVE.

So then we all tried to guess what it is. Here are our Top Seven guesses:

Guesser	Guess	Chance of being correct (with reasons)
 ME	A famous celebrity (like my favourite pop singer, Cassi Valentine!) is coming to our school.	**99.9%**  Please, please, please, please, pretty please be true!
 ZOE	We are getting a horse to be our class pet. 	**50%**  We had baby chicks last year, and a horse is just another type of farm animal.  Although where would it sit? 

Guesser	Guess	Chance of being correct (with reasons)
	We are going to stop being a real school and become a pirate school instead, and everyone is going to learn cool stuff like how to draw treasure maps and say 'Arrrr'.	**5%** Mr Martini would NEVER let this happen. Though I do like the idea of drawing treasure maps.

ARRRRRR!

Raf

Everyone in our class is going to Mars with our own personal jet packs.

0%

Anyone with even a tiny brain knows that there are no shops or oxygen on Mars and we would ALL DIE!!!

Peter

All the teachers at our school (including the principal, Mr Martini) have turned into zombies and have to go to a special zombie treatment facility to be un-zombified.

0%

If our teachers were really zombies, according to the Rules of Zombiedom, we'd all be zombies by now too!

Guesser	Guess	Chance of being correct (with reasons)
	Our school is going to close down for the next two weeks! 	**0.1%** This is just silly. Unless all the toilets blew up. (But then again we'd already know if that happened!)
 Zac	Our school is going to close down for the next two years!!! 	**0.0000000001%** This is even sillier. It would never take that long to fix the toilets, even if they were smashed into teeny tiny pieces.

Ms Weiss said all our guesses were wrong. But then she said one of them was actually VERY CLOSE to the REAL thrilling and mysterious thing!

And she was just about to tell us what it was when the bell started ringing!

And sirens started blaring!

And all the little kids from the baby classes ran out into the playground screaming their heads off, while Mrs Gupta and Mr Bing tried to herd them into lines.

And then Mrs Cardamone ran along the corridor with a megaphone saying, '**Fire Drill! Fire Drill!** Please make your way to the covered area and wait with your class.'

And we all had to hold hands with a partner like BABIES and walk out quietly to the covered area and line up in rows.

~~Unforch~~ Unfortunately, some of the boys from my class (especially Peter and Raf) thought this would be a really good time to start behaving like zombies. They made their eyes roll around in their eye sockets and said things like 'Brains, brains!' and clutched each other's throats like zombies do.

Ms Weiss was **NOT** amused. So as soon as the fire drill finished and we all came back to class, she made us do a spot spelling test with extra hard words in it, like **RESPONSIBLE** and **RELIABLE** and **SENSIBLE** and ~~MACHEWER~~ **MATURE**, until the *real* bell went for the end of school.

So I **STILL** don't know what the **thrilling** and **mysterious** thing is. Or which of the seven ideas was the very close one.

I hope it was mine!!!

Or Zoe's!!

Or maybe it is both of them mixed up together, and Cassi Valentine is going to come to our school on a horse and give us all horseriding lessons!

I can't wait to FIND OUT

Good night, Diary.
Sweet dreams.
Ella xx

Tuesday, after school

Dear Diary,

Ms Weiss FINALLY told us the thrilling and mysterious news this morning.

We're going to be doing a SCHOOL PLAY this term! And she and Mr Zugaro (my second-most favouritest teacher, because he likes my poetry) are going to be organising it. YAY!!!

I love school plays. I was just about to put up my hand and tell Ms Weiss how happy I was about the play, when Precious Princess Peach Parker, who is the most annoying person in the history of annoyingness and also a SUPER SUCKY teacher's pet, put up her hand and said, 'Oooooooooo. We're so LUCKY! I LOVE being in school plays. What's it going to be about, Ms Weiss?'

And then Ms Weiss gave Princess Peach one of her special smiles, which is SOOO unfair, because it should have been ME who got the special smile. ☹

And then she turned back to the class and said, 'Remember how I said one of the guesses you made yesterday was VERY CLOSE?'

And then Peter and Raf called out, 'Zombies! Yesss!'

They were just jumping up to do their zombie dance again when they saw the look on Ms Weiss's face and said, 'Oops. Sorry, Miss.' Then they sat down again before she gave us another spelling test.

Then Ms Weiss said that, actually, the play wasn't going to be about zombies. Or us going to Mars with our own personal jet packs. Or the school closing down. Or a class-pet horse.

It was going to be about . . .

Drum roll . . .

Pirates

We're going to do a play set on a pirate ship, with lots of singing and dancing, called Pirates of the Cariboboo.

There's going to be a piratical pirate called Captain Swashbuckler, who is the Scourge* of the Seven Seas.

* A 'scourge' is something that causes great trouble or suffering. Like a pesky mosquito with giganterous bitey parts. Or Olivia, my little sister. You say it like this—skerrj.

There's also a fantabulously fabulous character in the play called Mabel Diggs that I would be **PERFECT** for!

She sings. ✓

And dances. ✓

And does piratey stuff like sword fighting. ✓

And Ms Weiss said the girl who plays Mabel gets to wear lots of different super-stylish costumes. ✓✓✓

I have to be Mabel. I just HAVE to!

And besides all the main piratey roles, there are going to be ship's rats, and a ship's cat called Tiddles to chase them, and a talking parrot named Polly.

Here is a list of the main characters:

Pirates of THE CARIBOOBOO CHARACTER LIST:

CAPTAIN Swashbuckler
THE SCOURGE OF THE SEVEN SEAS

Mabel Diggs
A MYSTERIOUS MEMBER OF THE CREW

Tommy KNUCKLE
the FIRST MATE that has a heart of gold

DENNIS DOOLITTLE
a lazy pirate

DENISE DOOLITTLER
another lazy pirate

POLLY
THE PARROT

TIDDLES
THE SHIP'S CAT

It's going to be **excellently excellent**. I can't wait!

I have to stop writing now, Diary, because Zoe is coming over so we can have an

EMERGENCY meeting

about the play, and I haven't made the **KEEP OUT** sign for my bedroom door yet.

If I don't make the sign, Olivia will think she can come in again and start rearranging things on my desk. And my bookshelves. And repeat everything we say (including our most secretest secrets) to her friend Matilda, who will then blab our secrets to all her friends, **JUST LIKE SHE DID LAST TIME!**

Bye.

Love, Ella

Tuesday, after school, fifteen minutes later

Still waiting for Zoe to turn up.

Here is a picture of the sign I made. I used three different gel pens. It's the best one ever! ☺☺☺

Tuesday night, after dinner

Dearest Diary,

Zoe finally turned up! Phew. When we were absolutely totally completely utterly 100% sure that Olivia wasn't snooping on us by sitting on the other side of the door with a drinking glass, we started our meeting.

This is what we said:

Me: Pirates of the Caribooboo is going to be **EXcellent**.

Zoe: I know.

Me: You and I are **PERFECT** for this play. We're both going to get main roles for sure.

Zoe: I know. It's so exciting!

Me (casually): Which part are you going for?

Me (silently, inside my brain):
Please don't say Mabel.
Please don't say Mabel.
Please don't say Mabel.

Zoe: Maybe one of the animals? Like Tiddles the Cat? I don't want one of the big speaking parts. What if I forget my lines on stage? It would be sooo embarrassing!

Me (inside my brain again): *Phew.*

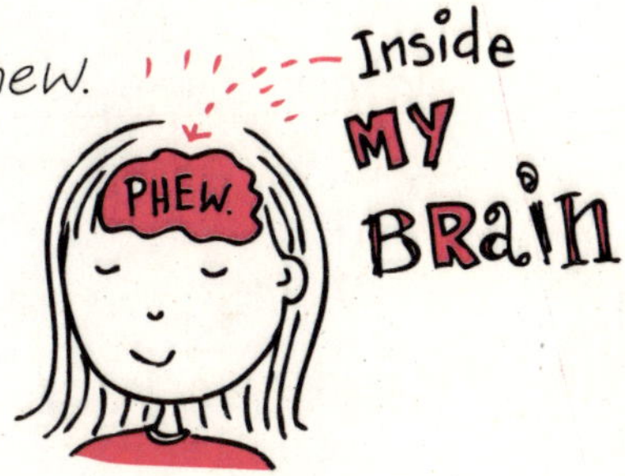

Zoe: What about you?

Me: Mabel. In fact, I am desperatingly desperate to be Mabel. I hope we get lots of scenes together.

Zoe: Same.

We were in the middle of planning our thank-you speeches (for when people come up onto the stage at the end of the play to give us flowers) when we heard a muffled noise, which sounded ~~suspish~~ suspiciously like

Olivia dropping a glass on the carpet outside my door, and then someone saying 'Oops'.

This is what happened next:

Me: I can hear you out there, O-liv-ia.
Muffled sound: Nnmnoyoomnncannt.
Me: Yes I can. You're SNOOPING on us.
Muffled sound: Nnmnolmmnmnot.
Me: YES YOU ARE! Now STOP BEING A PAIN AND **GO AWAY!**
Olivia: I'm **SOOO** telling Mum on you!

Sisters! They are **SOOOO** infuriating!

After that Zoe and I didn't feel like planning thank-you speeches anymore. So we had fun doing piratey things like practising our 'Arrrrs' and dancing the sailor's hornpipe* instead.

* The hornpipe is a type of jumpy dance that sailors do, with folded arms and lots of kickerous leg moves.

And then we dressed Bob up like a pirate. Here is a picture of what he looked like. Doesn't he look sweet?

I am **SO LUCKY** to have a BFF like Zoe. I wish she was my sister. Then she could live here all the time and I'd never be annoyed or infuriated or snooped on ever again.

Good night, Diary.
Talk tomorrow.
E xx

Wednesday night, just before lights out

Hey, Diary,

Guess what? Today we found out some more interesting facts about the Mysterious Amethyst Merryweather.

INTERESTING FACTS ABOUT AMETHYST

1 She LOVES reading and always has her nose in a book. Especially at lunchtime, when everyone else is running madly around the playground like mad things.

2 She doesn't like sandwiches. (I discovered this when I kindly offered her one of my ~~gormay~~ gourmet chicken liver with chopped egg and beetroot sandwiches at lunchtime today—so she wouldn't feel so lonely and new—and she went all pale and looked like she was going to throw up.)

3 She always wears something that is purple, like a hair ribbon or shoelaces. Cordelia (who also loves reading and knows lots of interesting stuff) says this is

because amethysts are ~~jools~~ jewels that are purple.

AMETHYST = PURPLE jewel

4 She must get into trouble A LOT.* I saw her sitting outside Mr Martini's office THREE WHOLE TIMES this week. And she didn't look happy when I asked her why she was sitting there. Especially the THIRD time I asked her.

* It must be for doing something like running in the school corridor or writing rude words on the wall in the girls' toilets because she NEVER EVER gets into trouble in class. Ever.

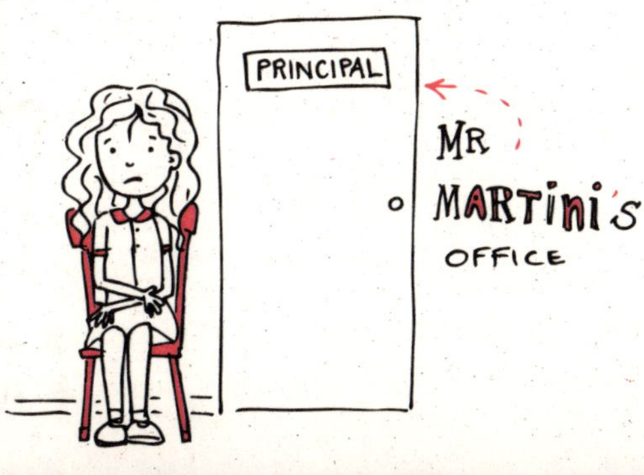

And guess what else?
The auditions for the play start on Monday!
We're going to get our scripts tomorrow and we have to choose a part and practise saying some of our lines. Then at the audition we will read them out in front of the part-chooserers.

I am going to practise my lines ALL WEEKEND!

Good night, Diary.
Love, Ella xx

Thursday morning, very, very early

Dear Diary,

I just had the best dream!

We were doing the play and I was Mabel and I had my own private, personal dressing room with a star on the door, like this:

And people kept walking past and leaving me giganterous bunches of flowers

and there were newspaper and TV reporters wanting to interview me

and thousands of people were screaming out my name

and lining up to get my autograph.

It was aMAZing.

Love, (Celebrity) Ella

Friday morning, early

Guess what? I had the dream about being Mabel AGAIN!

Maybe this means it's all going to come true. I CAN'T WAIT!!

Friday night, late

Dear Diary,

I am so ANGRY I want to SCREAM!

Really, really LOUDLY!!

Like this!

This is what happened at school today.

Zoe and I were quietly working on our Famous Pirates through History projects,* and I was telling her all about my aMAZing dreams. And I was up to the part about how everyone wanted my autograph when I heard this sniggery, snorty sound right beside me.

* Ms Weiss thought it would be fun to do pirate projects in class because of our school play. Mine's about this lady river pirate from the olden days called Sadie the Goat.

And guess who it was?

Perfect Princess Peach Parker. She was standing next to our table with a big sneery smirk all over her face.

So I said, 'Can I help you?'

And she said, 'I don't know. Can you?'

Then she handed me this scratchy, old glitter pen THAT WASN'T EVEN MINE and said in this really fakey voice, 'I found this on the floor, and while I've been waiting for you to stop talking so I could give it to you, I accidentally overheard you telling Zoe how you're going to be Mabel in the play.'

And then before I could say anything, she looked down her nose at me and said, 'Ha! Like that's ever going to happen,' and went back to her friends.

Peach is such a SNOOP! And a MEANIE! I sat there staring straight ahead, getting furiouser and furiouser, thinking of all the things I wanted to say to her.

Zoe put her arm around me and said, 'Don't listen to her, Ella. You can be **anything** you want to be and she can't stop you.'

And then she showed me this really fancy way to do a heading for my **Sadie the Goat** project, with little curly goat horns coming out of the G.

And then I helped her write a funny poem about her pirate, Blackbeard.

Blackbeard's beard
Was really weird
And darker than the night
He looked into a mirror once
And gave himself a fright!

And then we told each other funny pirate jokes, like:

Q. What is a pirate's favourite subject at pirate school?

A. ARRRRT!

and

Q. What are pirates afraid of?

A. THE DAAAAAAARK!

and

Q. Why are pirates called pirates?

A. They just ARRRRRR!

And then we kept saying ARRRRRRRRR! over and over and we laughed and laughed till we got tummy aches and our faces hurt, and Ms Weiss had to tell us to stop being silly and get on with our work.

Laughing and being silly with Zoe made me feel A LOT betterer.

But I still want to SCREAM!!!!

☹☹☹

Saturday night, just before lights out

Dear Diary-doo,

Guess what?!

Nanna Kate took Zoe and me to the movies at the shopping centre today as a special treat for helping her with the weeding. (Nanna Kate HATES weeding. Especially when she finds squished snails on the stalks with bits of their guts hanging out. Eww.)

Unfortunately, Olivia and Max came along too, even though they didn't do any weeding. It's **SO UNFAIR!**

Zoe and I **REALLY** wanted to see the new pirate movie called **The Pirate Princess**, but Max made us late because he kept stopping all the time to look at bugs, and by the time we got there it was **SOLD OUT!**

So we had to see this BABY movie made for BABIES instead.

When the movie finished Zoe and I went to the food court, while Nanna Kate took Olivia and Max to the toilet so they'd stop whining about wanting to wee all the time. (Everyone kept looking at us while they were doing the whining. It was SO EMBARRASSING!)

And guess what?

You never will so I'll just tell you.

We accidentally bumped into Peach at the ice-cream shop. NOOOOOOOOOOOOOOOOOO!

She was with her best buddies, Jade and Prinny.

They were all wearing matchy-matchy outfits. Even their ice-creams were matchy.

BLEUCHhh.

'Oh, look,' said Peach (fake) sweetly to her friends. 'It's Mould-y May-belle.'

And then they all laughed like hyenas who had caught a laughing disease.

Zoe glared at them glaringly. Then she said, 'What's your problem? Ella can be Mabel if she wants to.'

Peach gave me one of her creepy crocodile smiles. Then she came up really close to me, so close I could practically see up her nose. Eww.

This is what we all said next:

Peach: I hope you know all your lines, Mould-y May-belle.

Me: What do you mean?

Zoe: Yeah, what do you mean?

Peach: You have to know all your lines **off by heart** for the audition.

Prinny: Yeah.

Jade: Yeah.

Zoe: No we don't. We can just read them off the script. Ms Weiss said.

Peach: That's what EVERYONE ELSE who wants to be Mabel will be doing.

Me: So?

Peach (moving in even closer): But if you REALLY want the part, you have to do something extra to show you're more specialler than them.

Me (suspiciously): Are you learning your lines?

Peach (innocently): Of course! Prinny and Jade have been helping me, haven't you, Prinny and Jade?

Prinny and Jade (together): Yeah.

Zoe (even more suspiciously): So which part are you going for?

Peach: Ummm . . . Denise Doodah. I mean Doodad. I mean Doolittler. Yeah, her. Anyway, we have to go now. Tootles!

Prinny and Jade (together): Yeah, tootles!

And then they walked off with smirky smirks all over their smirky faces.

I was just about to call another Emergency Meeting with Zoe to discuss what we should do about knowing our lines when Nanna Kate came back with Max and Olivia.

So we're going to have it tomorrow instead.

Love,
Ella x

Sunday, after dinner

Dear Diary,

Zoe and I spent the WHOLE DAY getting ready for our auditions tomorrow. It was the BEST Emergency Meeting in the history of Emergency Meetings!

Here's what we did:

1. Phoned Olivia's best friend Matilda and convinced her, with lollies and glitter pens, to invite Olivia over to her house, so she couldn't snoop on us again.

2 Practised our sword fighting.

3 Talked like pirates in piratey voices.

4. Said our lines from the play over and over AND OVER again until we knew them off by heart. Mine were MUCH harder to remember than Zoe's.

Goodnight, Diary.

Ella

xoxox

Sunday night, very late

Dearest Diary,

I am WAY too excited about the auditions to sleep. So I wrote this shape poem about being a star instead.

A

star

twinkles

and shines

in the sky and

lights up the world.

Star light star bright here's the wish I wish tonight:

I wish I could be Mabel in the school play and

sing and act and dance and have a star

on my dressing room door and

people would clap and cheer

and bring me flowers.

A star glows and gleams

and brings joy to everyone.

I want to be a shining star!

A glistening glimmering

sparkly glittery

shiny star.

Wish me good luck for tomorrow, Diary!

Love,
Ella xoxox

Monday, straight after school

Dear Diary,

I am **SHOCKED!**

So shocked I can't write anything about what happened right now.

Maybe later, after I've had a nice calming walk with Bob in the park.

In disguise. In case I bump into someone I don't want to see or talk to.

E

Monday, about half an hour later

Nope. Still too shocked to write.

Monday, about ten minutes after that

Maybe I'll be able to write something after dinner—if I am still alive then. I may have died of an extreme case of Desperating Despair Disease. The one that makes all your teeth and toenails and heart fall out. At least then I will have an ~~exyou~~ excuse not to go to school tomorrow.

Because I am never EVER going back to school.

Ever.

☹☹☹☹

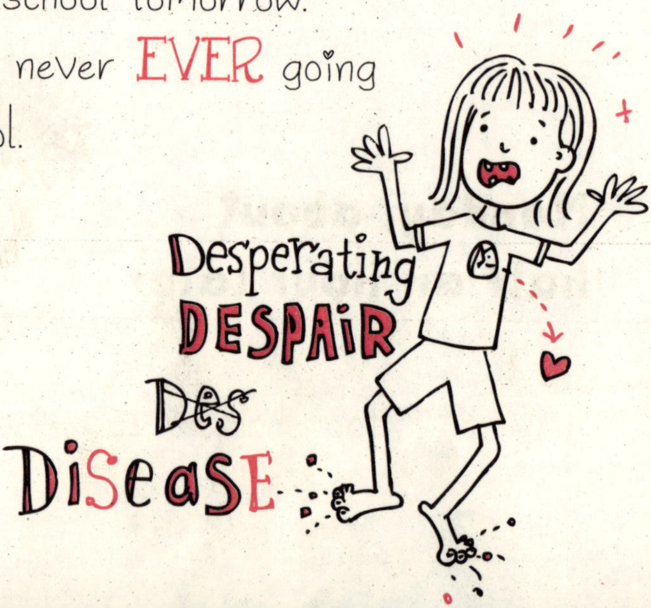

Monday night, in bed

Dearest Diary,

Max came in just now with a comforting hot water bottle, plus half* an old stale Easter egg he found at the back of his toy cupboard, and gave them to me because he thought I looked sad.

* Max already ate the other half.

Maybe I can write a little bit about what happened today.

WARNING: This next bit is exTREMEly sad and tragical. You may need tissues.

Zoe and I arrived at school super early so we could write our names on the auditions list before it filled up with other people wanting the same parts as us.

Pirates of THE CAriboooboo
AUDITIONS
Where : Ethel Morman Memorial Gym
When : 1:15 pm SHARP!
Please write your name here:
Daniel Ratcliffy
Peach Parker
Prinny Aquino
Harry Spotter
Jade Snyder
Johnno Depp

We added our names then ran off to our **special place** under the cypress trees to do some more practising.

When school finally started, Ms Weiss had to tell us both **THREE TIMES** to 'settle down please'. But we were too fizzy with **EXCITEMENT**. We couldn't wait for it to be lunchtime so we could show the directors how **FANTABULOUSLY FABULOUS** we were!

At lunchtime, we went to the gym at 1.15 pm sharp, just like the notice said. But . . .

Da da da . . .

Dummmmmmm.

There was nobody there.

Precious Princess Peach Parker had tricked us.

AGAIN!

The notice was FAKE! FAKE! FAKE!

Even the names on it were FAKE!

Harry Spotter doesn't even go to our school. How emBARRassing! Anyone with even a tiny brain knows that!

So then we ran madly around the school like mad things, trying to find out where the REAL audition place was before lunchtime finished and we missed out on being Mabel and Tiddles forever. ☹

We were just about to give up and spend the rest of our lives in desperating despair when we saw Cordelia coming out of a room with a sign on it that said:

And guess what?

The auditions were still going!

You're probably thinking that everything that happened after that was fantabulously fabulous and there was a happy ending, just like in a fairytale.

WRONG! WRONG! WRONG!

There was no happy ending.

In fact it was the **sadderest** ending in the history of endings. ☹☹☹☹

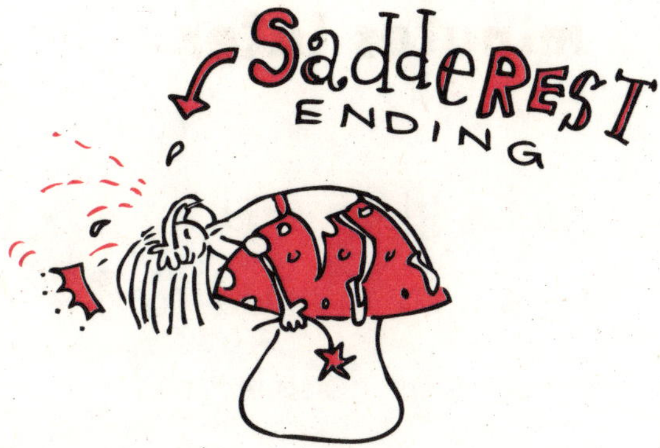

I have to stop for a bit now, so I can get some more tissues. And maybe some chocolate-chip cookies. And some ice-cream—with chocolate sprinkles. I'll be right back . . .

Monday night, about two minutes later

Sadly, Mum said I was only allowed to have one cookie and no ice-cream (with or without sprinkles), because all that rich food so close to bedtime would be bad for me and might give me nightmares.

That is SO unfair!

I bet Princess Peach is allowed to have ice-cream (with sprinkles!) any time she wants.* ☹

* Actually, I hope she does have ice-cream and does have nightmares. Scary ones with big hairy, googly-eyed monsters in them. (I know that makes me sound mean, but I am too ~~DISTRORT~~ DISTRAUGHT to care anymore.)

So back to the story . . . Zoe and I sat down on the chairs, waiting for it to be our turn, watching all the other kids reading out bits of the play.

Most of them were **hopelessly hopeless**, ~~exp~~ especially Don Tay.* Don Tay is this boy who was in our class at ballet school. In fact, he was the *only* boy in our class at ballet school. He was also the only boy at the auditions, which means he is guaranteed 100% sure to get a part. It's so not fair. ☹

* His real name is actually Dante, but we didn't know that until we saw it on a list one day. Oops!

But guess what? There was one girl who was exCEPTionally excellent at actoring. She was so good everyone stopped whispering to each other and thinking When's it going to be MY turn? and stared at her with shiny eyes and said, 'Zow-ee, she is aMAZing.'

Guess who it was? You never will in a million gatrillion years, so I'll just tell you.

It was Amethyst Merryweather! She is what my Nanna Kate calls a dark horse.** Which makes her EVEN MORE mysterious. I wonder how she got so good at actoring?

** A dark horse isn't actually a horse at all. It is a person who everyone thinks is hopelessly hopeless at something, like playing the bagpipes or winning spitting competitions, but they are in fact fantabulously fabulous at it and everyone says 'Ooo! What a big surprise. I am SHOCKED.'

All that sitting and waiting made me more and more nerverous. I was so nerverous there were butterflies doing the cancan in my tummy.

And then all of a sudden Ms Weiss called out Zoe's name and asked her which part she wanted to be. And Zoe got mixed up and said 'Miaow?' instead of 'Tiddles, the ship's cat'.

And everybody laughed.

Then Zoe did a few more miaows and pretended to do that thing cats do when they lick their paws then rub them behind their ears, and then she pranced around like a real cat and everyone laughed again. Especially Ms Weiss and Mr Zugaro, who had giganterous smiles on their faces the whole time she was acting and kept giving each other 'meaningful looks', like this:

Amethyst gave Zoe a **giganterous smile** as well, like it was the **best thing** she'd ever seen.

And then Zoe sat down again with a big 'PHEWW' and it was my turn.

Mr Zugaro gave me a script to read from but I said, 'No thank you very much, I don't need one. I know my part by heart.'

And then something **horrifically horrible** happened. So **horrifically horrible** I wanted the floor to open up so I could disappear down into the deep, dark ground so no-one could ever see me again. Not even if they had a torch on their head, like miners do.

So **horrifically horrible** I can hardly write it down, because then it will be true.

I forgot my lines. ☹

Everyone was staring at me, waiting for me to start. But I couldn't remember Mabel's speech, even though I'd practised it with Zoe about 900 times. So I made something up instead.

Mabel's speech (the real one)

I'm Mabel Diggs from Violet Town,
A sassy lass, that's me.
A pirate's life is all I want,
So I ran away to sea.

What I ~~Ack~~ Actually Said

Hello, my name is Mabel Piggs and I . . .
(mumble mumble) . . . I like . . . umm . . .
pirate stuff. And running.

And then everybody laughed. Only it wasn't nice, friendly laughing, like they did when Zoe was being a cat. It was **mean, horrid, horrible, NASTY** laughing.

And guess who was laughing the **nastierest?**

HINT: Her name rhymes with speech.

Princess Peach is a **LIAR, LIAR, PANTS ON FIRE.**

She didn't know her part off by heart either. She just read her lines from the script, like all the other people auditioning.

It was all just a big, mean, nasty-pasty TRICK to make me look bad.

And guess which part she tried out for?

HINT: It rhymes with table.

NOOOOOOOOOO!

Why, Diary? WHY?????

Tuesday, after school

Dear Diary,

I am **STILL** shocked!

Ms Weiss and Mr Zugaro put up a 'callback' list of people they wanted to see again before they decided on the main parts.

Zoe's name was on the list.

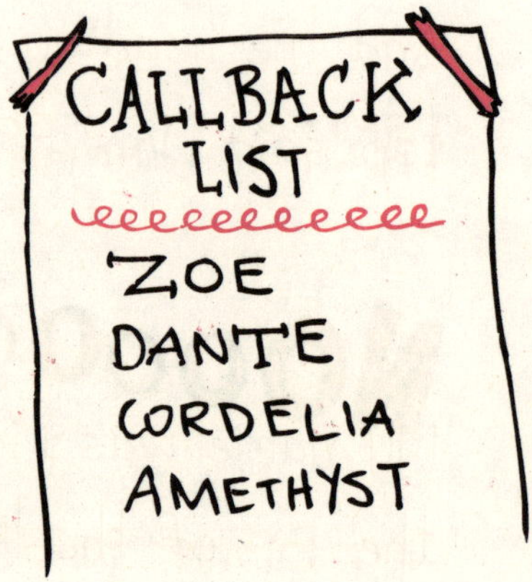

And Don Tay's.
And Cordelia's.
And Mysterious Amethyst's.

Mine wasn't.

I was just about to creep away to die a slow and lingering tragical desperating death under the cypress trees when Zoe discovered another list, right next to the first one.

And the heading at the top said DANCERS.

The Good News

My name was right at the top of the list!

The Bad News

Princess Peach's name was right underneath mine. And so were Prinny's and Jade's. And then the names of all the gym girls who do gymnastics at lunchtimes, with their hair pulled back into tight little buns—in case it gets caught in the gym equipment and then their heads EXPLODE.

The Not So Bad News That Made Me Feel a Bit Betterer

And then underneath their names were the names of my other friends, like Georgia and Chloe and Daisy and Poppy. So we are all going to be dancers in the play together. YAY!

But it's SO NOT FAIR, Diary. I really, really, REALLY wanted to be Mabel.

And now someone else is going to be her instead.

AND IT'S ALL PEACH PARKER'S FAULT!

Wednesday night, in bed, just before lights out

Dear Diary,

Today was the ~~worserest~~ worst day of my life.

EVER!!

Here's what happened.

I went with Zoe to the callbacks, even though I was desperatingly sad that my two favouritest teachers in the WHOLE WORLD hadn't chosen me—because that is the kind of thing BFFs do. And because I was happy for Zoe that she'd been chosen, even though I was SEETHING with ENVY. (And also because Ms Weiss said there were going to be snacks.)

Mr Zugaro called up all the callback people one by one to read the different parts. Then he and Ms Weiss asked us to wait quietly (ha!) while they had a BIG DISCUSSION.

While we were waiting (un)quietly, Amethyst came over. Amethyst! The same Amethyst who never speaks. Ever.

This is what we* said:

* ~~Achsh~~ Actually, this is what Amethyst and Zoe said. I didn't get a chance to say ANYthing.

Amethyst: Hey, Zoe. You were really good.
Zoe (going all red): Umm, no I wasn't.
Everyone laughed.
Amethyst: Because you were REALLY FUNNY. You were aMAZing.

Zoe (going all redder): ☺

Amethyst: You should have gone for one of the main parts, like Denise or Mabel.

Zoe (shocked): No way! I'd muck up all my lines.

Amethyst: No you wouldn't. You'd be great! I think—

Sadly, we never did get to find out what Amethyst thinks, because Ms Weiss and Mr Zugaro finished their big discussion, and said they were ready to give out the main parts. All the actors stopped being (un)quiet and stood there, staring up at them with shiny eyes, waiting to find out if they got one.

EVERYone thought Don Tay would get Captain Swashbuckler, the mainest of all the main parts.

But guess what? He didn't. Amethyst did! Don Tay will be Tommy Knuckle instead.

And guess which part Zoe got?

(If you guessed Tiddles the Cat you are

WRONG!

WRONG!

WRONG!)

★MABEL★

She was shocked! But also really happy.

Then all the people with main parts had to line up so Ms Weiss could take their photo.

And then they stayed there chatting and having fun when the bell rang and everyone else (including me ☹) had to go back to class.

Good night, Diary.
E

Thursday, after school

Dear Diary,

Today we started our dance rehearsals with Ms Crosby. I was hoping Zoe might come to watch like I did for her, but she said she would be too busy with her OWN rehearsal. With the ACTors.

And then she said,

So that's OK then.

OUR rehearsal was **EXcellent!**

There are two groups of dancers.

Group A

Group A (the best dancers) are the crew of the pirate ship. They are going to do lots of **complicated dances** with ropes and mops and even **sword fighting!** And one dancer gets to do a special dance called a pas de deux* with one of the actors!

* A *pas de deux* is a dance for two people. You say it like this—pah de der. I learned how to dance them at ballet school. You do leaps and twirls and arabesques where you stick your back leg up really high in the air.

Group B

Group B (the not-so-good dancers) are the ship's rats. They are going to do a funny dance where they get chased around the deck by Tiddles.

We all held our breath and crossed our fingers and toes while we waited for Ms Crosby to tell us which group we were in.

The Good News

I'm in **GROUP A**

The Bad News

So are Princess Peach and Prinny and Jade and all the stuck-up gym-bun girls. ☹

The Badderer News

All my second-best friends like Georgia and Poppy and Daisy and Chloe are in Group B. Which means I won't have anyone to have fun with when we're rehearsing. ☹☹☹

Then Ms Crosby said there is going to be an extra-special dancing audition to see who gets to dance the pah de der.

I really, really want to win!

I have to go now so I can practise my leaps and twirls and arabesques for tomorrow.

Wish me luck, Diary!

Love,

Ella xx

Thursday, about fifteen minutes later

Dear Diary,

Well, I just rang Zoe to see if she wanted to come over to my house to help me practise for the pah de der auditions. And guess what? She said she couldn't because she was already doing something with ANOTHER FRIEND.

So I had to practise my pah de der with a chair. ☹☹☹

Friday night, in bed

Dear, darlingest Diary,

We had the pah de der auditions today and we all had to do a really tricky dance to show off our ~~teckneek~~ technique. I wore my best tutu and did a dance I learnt at ballet school. It looked like this:

This time the butterflies in my stomach were doing the cha-cha-cha. I really, REALLY wanted Zoe to be there to watch me dance for good luck but she just smiled a little smile and said, 'Sorry, Ella, not today. I have a big scene to rehearse with someone else.'

What???!

But guess what?

Ms Crosby chose ME to do the pah de der, even without Zoe's good luck!

Not Peach, or Prinny or Jade.

ME!

And I get to change out of the boring stripy T-shirt and baggy pants and bandana that all the ship's crew wear and into a stylish floaty costume for my special dance.

It is going to be AWESOME!

Except for one tiny problem.

The person I am dancing the pah de der with is . . .

Last time Don Tay danced a pah de der it was with Esther Grech in our ballet concert, and he got all tangled up in her floaty dress when he picked her up and twirled her around over his head. And then he dropped her and Esther broke her big toe in two places and had to go to hospital in an ~~amber~~ ambulance.

WAAAAHhh!

Good night,

Ella

Saturday night, in bed, very late

Dear Diary,

I am in desperating despair.
☹

I called Zoe this morning to see if she wanted to come over so we could work on ideas for my floaty costume for my big dance scene. Zoe always has excellently excellent ideas for things like that.

Her mum said she'd gone to the movies WITH A FRIEND and she was going to be out ALL DAY but maybe we could catch up tomorrow. And she would get Zoe to call me back.

And I said (casually), 'Oh that's nice. Did she say what movie?'

And her mum said, 'Yes, she did. It was a lovely movie all about pirates called The Pirate Princess.'

The movie I wanted to see last Saturday. With Zoe. My BFF.

☹☹☹☹☹☹☹☹

Saturday night, a bit later

Which friend??????

Sunday, after lunch

I waited ALL morning for Zoe to call me back.

She didn't.

Zoe and I always call each other at least 900 times on the weekend. EsPECially on Sunday mornings. ☹

I must be the only person in the WHOLE WORLD who doesn't have someone to talk to. I couldn't even talk to Olivia because she was HAVING FUN at her friend Matilda's house. ALL DAY.

I am stuck in my room dying of boredness, Diary! In fact I am SO BORED I am extremely surprised my head hasn't exploded.

So I worked on ideas for my costume with Max.

Yours in desperation,

Ella

PS He wasn't very helpful.

Sunday evening, just before dinner

Dear Diary,

Everything is hopelessly hopeless. I am so devastatingly distraught I think I might die a slow and tragical death extremely soon. (Though probably not till after dinner because we are having spaghetti, my favourite.)

Here is a list of things I am bequeathing* to my family and (ex)BFFs after I die:

Name	What I am bequeathing them
 Dad	Gerald, my (latest) pet praying mantis 
 Mum	My butterfly hairclips 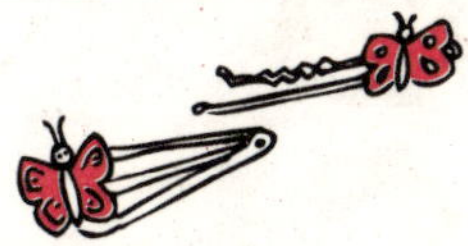
 Olivia	My gel and glitter pen collection (except for the mauve, pink and purple ones. She is NEVER getting those. Ever.) 
 Max	Barnaby B Bear, my favourite one-eyed teddy 
 Nanna Kate	The 'My Secret' perfume she gave me for my birthday two years ago (there is still quite a lot left in the bottle)

Name	What I am bequeathing them
BOB	My red shoes that he is always trying to chew up 
Peach	(ex) BFF Nothing
ZOE	(ex) BFF An even bigger nothing

* 'Bequeathing' means giving stuff to people that you won't need because you'll be too dead to use it.

I'm too distressed to write any more now, Diary. Maybe after dinner, if I am feeling strong enough.

Ella x

Sunday night, in bed

Dear Diary,

I am eating some chocolate biscuits I found in the pantry. Who cares if I have nightmares (even ones with hairy, googly-eyed monsters in them)? My life is already a big nightmare RIGHT NOW.

Here's what happened.

I was taking Bob for a nice relaxing walk in the park today when I saw something Extremely Suspicious over near the ornamental fountain.

I immediately went into ninja stealth mode and hid behind a giant tree so I could Observe the Suspicious Behaviour without being seen.*

* which is extremely hard to do when you are holding a very bouncy, very licky dog so he won't bark and reveal your location or run over to the person who is Behaving Suspiciously.

And guess who I Observed???

Zoe. Chatting and laughing and trying on silly hats with her New Friend.

Zoe doesn't even **like** wearing hats.

And guess who her **New Friend** is???

HINT: Her name is a type of ~~jool~~ jewel.

Monday, after school

Dear Diary,

I wish to announce that Zoe is now officially my ex-BFF.

That is all.

Monday, about twelve minutes later

~~It's Because~~

Monday, about twenty minutes after that

~~It's because she doesn't want to be my~~

Monday, about two minutes after that

Sooo—here's what happened.

When I got to school this morning Zoe was waiting for me in our special spot near the cypress trees, just like everything was **absolutely, completely, utterly, totally OK** and she hadn't spent practically the **WHOLE WEEKEND** being a **traitorous traitor** instead of a true and loyal BFF.

There was so much I wanted to talk about with her. Like how **excitered** and **happy** I was when Ms Crosby chose me to do the pah de der. And how she was going learning all her lines. And how worried I was that I might make a mistake in my dance. Or that Don Tay might drop me. ☹

Here's what we said instead:

Zoe (brightly): Hi, Ella!
How was your weekend?
Me: Did you just say something?
Zoe (puzzled): Huh?

Me: Ohhhh. So you're talking to me then.

Zoe (even more puzzled): Sure. (Pausing to wave back to her special New Friend, who was waving at her from the other side of the downball courts.) Why wouldn't I be?

Me: Why don't you just go away and leave me alone? You've obviously got more exciting things to do OVER THERE.

Zoe (checking her watch to see how much time was left before the bell went): Well, if you're sure? Ammy was going to go over my lines with me. We've got a really important rehearsal at lunchtime today.

Me (inside my brain): Ammy???

Me (out loud): One gatrillion per cent sure. And you know what? You don't HAVE to be my BFF anymore.

Zoe: What? What are you talking about?

Me: You know EXACTLY what I'm talking about, Zo-ee.

Zoe: I do?

Me: Just forget we were ever friends, OK? You can be Ammy's BFF instead.

Zoe (rolling her eyes): You know what? I will.

Me: FINE!

Zoe: FINE!

And then we both stormed off like storming thunderstorms and we didn't say ONE WORD to each other for the WHOLE REST OF THE DAY.

Tuesday, after school

Still not speaking to Zoe.

Wednesday, after dinner

Still not speaking.

NOPE.

NOPE.

NOPE.

Thursday, after school

The phone rang and I raced to get it in case it was Zoe calling me to say sorry, but it was only Matilda calling to see if Olivia wanted to come over to play dollies. Bleuchhhh. Matilda and Olivia are such BABIES.

And anyway even if Zoe DID call to say sorry, I wouldn't say sorry back.

Not in a MILLION GATRILLION YEARS.

Wednesday night, in bed, exhausterated

Dearest Diary,

I'm so sorry I haven't written in you for a whole week but I have been busy busy busy—like a busy bumblebee buzzing around, getting ready for our play.

Guess what happened today!

Princess Peach was being a BIG SHOW-OFF while we were practising our rope-climbing dance. She climbed up to the top of the climbing frame in the gym and fell off and hurt her ankle. And now she can't be in the play.

I couldn't WAIT to tell Zoe all about it!

And then I remembered she's not my BFF anymore. So I didn't. ☹

Thursday night, in bed

Dear Diary,

Today, after school, Don Tay and I went to see Madame Fry (my old ballet teacher) and she gave us a private personal pah de der lesson!

And Don Tay picked me up and twirled me over his head and he only **ALMOST** dropped me once.

So now I'm feeling a **WHOLE lot better** about our dance next week.

Good night, Diary.
Sweet dreams.
Ella xx

☺ ☺ ☺

Friday night, after dinner

I was at the shopping centre with Mum and Olivia after school today buying some new shoes when we bumped into Poppy and Georgia.

Poppy said she'd just seen Amethyst with a lady and two little girls that looked just like Amethyst (except they weren't wearing anything purple) in the Do Drop In Coffee Shoppe—and they were sitting with Mr Martini!

Zow-ee! I wonder if she's in trouble again???

As soon as I got home I raced into the kitchen and called Zoe to find out MORE INFORMATION.

And then I remembered Zoe and I aren't *ever* speaking to each other again. Ever. We don't even talk to each other in class, which is EXTREMELY hard to do when you are sitting at the same table for practically THE WHOLE DAY.

So I hung up before she had a chance to pick up. ☹

Sunday night, in bed, very late

Dear Diary,

I am desperatingly trying to go to sleep and I can't.

I miss Zoe—REALLY, REALLY badly.

Mum said I was being silly and I should have called her this morning and asked her to come over. But Zoe was probably busy, I thought.

Busy doing something with Ammy.

E

Monday night, late

Dear Diary,

I can't sleep again tonight but this time it's because I AM SO EXCITERATED!

We had our dress rehearsal for the play! Which means I FINALLY got to wear my stylish, floaty pah de der dress. And it is aMAZing! And BEAUTiful! And ~~GORJus~~ GORGeous! It makes me feel just like a (pirate) princess.

Even Amethyst told me it was amazing. And she wished me good luck for tomorrow night. (Zoe didn't. ☹)

We did a run-through* of the play.

* A 'run-through' means you practise the whole play with all the singing and dancing and actoring and costumes. It does NOT mean you run across the stage screaming like zombies with their heads cut off.

Amethyst was REALLY good. You could tell why the teachers chose her to be Captain Swashbuckler.

Zoe was good too. Except I could tell she was REALLY nerverous, because her right knee was shaking like the coconuts in a coconut tree when a big wind is blowing at them. Zoe's knee ALWAYS does that when she's nerverous.

I can't wait for tomorrow night!

Wednesday night, very late

Dearest Diary,

We did the play!

The actors acted and said 'Aaaaarrrrrr!' and 'Ahoy, me hearties' a lot.

And the dancers who were the ship's rats ran around the stage and made everyone laugh (especially when they accidentally on purpose bumped into each other).

After all my special dances with the Group A girls (except for Princess Peach, of course, who sat scowling in the audience with her foot up on a cushion), I did my pah de der with Don Tay. And he didn't drop me. Not even once!

And Nanna Kate gave Mr Zugaro some flowers to give to me on the stage. As if I was a REAL STAR! And I got to take a bow on stage with all the people with main parts.

And guess what?

You never will so I'll just tell you.

Just before the curtain went up, Zoe got stage fright and she was too scared to go on! Her right knee started shaking again, and her voice went all trembly, and her face went white, just like a giganterous marshmallow.

So I went over and patted her gently on the arm and whispered, 'Don't be scared, Zoe. You can do ANYTHING,' just like we were still BFFs.

And then I ran off to get ready for my first dance.

And guess what else?

Zoe stopped being nerverous and was really, really good. Ms Weiss said she was the best Mabel she'd ever seen. Ever.

PS (five minutes later)

Oops. I forgot to tell you.

Mr Martini is actually Amethyst Merryweather's DAD!

Poppy heard Mr Martini talking to Ms Weiss about Amethyst. And guess what? She had to leave her other school and come to ours! And then Poppy told Georgia and Georgia told Chloe and Chloe told me.

And her real WHOLE name is actually Amethyst Martini Merryweather!! OBVIOUSLY Amethyst doesn't want anyone to know that HER DAD is the SCHOOL PRINCIPAL. That would be just WEIRD.

But that explains EVERYTHING about why Ammy is SO mysTERious (and sits outside Mr M's office a lot, even though she NEVER gets in trouble).

I wonder if she needs another friend?

PPS (five minutes after that)

And guess what else?

Zoe and I both said a very sorryful sorry to each other. At exactly the same time.

And now we're talking to each other again.

ELLA Diaries

Read more of Ella's brilliant diary in

Double Dare You

Ballet Backflip

I ♥ Pets

Dreams come true

Christmas CHAOS

Pony School Showdown

WORST CAMP EVER

and look out for more coming soon!